YOUR LEGAL RIGHTS IN THE WORKPLACE

RYAN NAGELHOUT

ROSEN PUBLISHING

New York

Published in 2016 by The Rosen Publishing Group, Inc.
29 East 21st Street, New York, NY 10010

Copyright © 2016 by The Rosen Publishing Group, Inc.

First Edition

Expert Reviewer: Lindsay A. Lewis, Esq.

Library of Congress Cataloging-in-Publication Data

Nagelhout, Ryan, author.
Your legal rights in the workplace/Ryan Nagelhout.
    pages cm.—(Know your rights)
Includes bibliographical references and index.
ISBN 978-1-4777-8044-2 (library bound) — ISBN 978-1-4777-
8616-1 (pbk.) — ISBN 978-1-4777-8617-8 (6-pack)
1. Employee rights—United States. 2. Labor laws and legislation—
United States. 3. Industrial relations—United States. I. Title.
KF3457.N34 2015
342.73'0684—dc23

                                                        2014037711

Manufactured in the United States of America

CONTENTS

INTRODUCTION

etting your first job is an exciting time in your life. Whether it's a paper route or work at a fast-food restaurant, entering the workplace is one of the first steps to becoming an adult. Getting that first paycheck brings you into a world of disposable income and, hopefully, savings. A job also means a new place to meet people. New life experiences often mean lots of new rules to learn and understand, and following these rules is an important part of learning how to act properly in the workplace. The workplace is not just another version of school, and not following the rules can lead to real consequences.

These lessons don't always come easily, though. Learning what your rights and responsibilities are in the workplace can be the difference between a long, happy job experience or a struggle to maintain good working relationships with your superiors and peers. It's easy to get involved in a bad situation if you're not careful. Sometimes your own actions can get you into trouble if you're not aware of what's expected of you while on the job. Employers may also try to take advantage of your inexperience in the workplace. Dennise and Cherise Mofidi thought working at a Papa Murphy's restaurant in Oregon would be the perfect after-school job. The sixteen-year-old twins liked working the cash register and making pizzas for customers. Soon, though, the twins became uncomfortable with sexual comments male managers made about them.

At first they were confused. "Is this normal?" they asked one another. One day, a manager asked Dennise to send him pictures of her breasts. The girls then started to tell family and friends and asked what they should do. The

Working at a pizza restaurant is a common job for young workers first entering the workplace. However, any workplace can become the setting for inappropriate words or actions.

other managers at Papa Murphy's didn't do anything about the harassment. Should they just quit or keep working there despite the harassment?

After exploring their options, the Mofidi twins filed a complaint with the Oregon Bureau of Labor and Industries (BOLI). The process was long—about a year—but the Mofidis used the legal system and told others about their issues. They held protests and fought restaurant ownership through the system BOLI set up to investigate these issues. The two girls eventually settled with Papa Murphy's. While some settlements prevent plaintiffs from discussing a case publicly, this one did not, so the Modifi sisters continue to tell their story today.

The Mofidis' story is a reminder that there are ways to fight workplace harassment and protect your rights. No matter your situation, you are not alone. Not only do you have a variety of tools at your disposal to defend yourself, but there are a number of people and outlets you can contact to help you navigate what often can be a difficult experience in growing up.

Whether the aggressor or victim, within these pages you will learn about the resources and people who can help you if you commit or come in contact with sexual harassment or other workplace crimes. You will also learn how to diffuse potentially harmful situations in the workplace, as well as what resources you can consult if you have questions about crimes in the workplace.

CHAPTER 1

JOINING THE WORKFORCE

America in the early twentieth century had workplaces filled with child laborers. Children, sometimes five or younger, would work long hours in dangerous conditions. Many worked instead of going to school. Today, there are many laws to protect children from unfair labor practices.

Children can join the workforce at different ages depending on what job they are doing. According to federal law, someone thirteen or under can work as a babysitter, deliver newspapers, or, in some cases, work as an actor or performer. Children between fourteen and fifteen can work at amusement parks, movie theaters, and other retail stores as well as do some office work. Children between sixteen and seventeen can do any job that isn't considered hazardous, but they aren't allowed to drive on the job.

Teenagers as young as fourteen can work in movie theaters. Federal law sets the standard age for different workplaces based on many factors, including how hazardous the work is.

Once you are eighteen, there are no federal restrictions on job type or how many hours you can work. Each state does have its own special rules for different types of work, as well as special rules for workers of different ages.

WAGES AND HOURS

The Fair Labor Standards Act (FLSA) sets guidelines for most workers in the United States. Workers must make at least the federally set minimum wage. The FLSA also sets a forty-hour work week, with overtime pay (one and a half times regular salary) given to hourly workers if they work more than forty hours. Employees who are tipped, such as waiters, may make $2.13 per hour but their tips must at least match minimum wage. Specific states and cities set a higher minimum wage that businesses have to follow. For example, in 2014 the city of Seattle, Washington, raised its minimum wage to a "living wage" of $15 per hour.

There are also hour restrictions for workers based on age. Children fourteen or fifteen years old can only work after 7 AM and until 7 PM each day, or until 9 PM from June 1 to Labor Day. Children under the age of eighteen can only work three hours per day on a school day and up to eighteen hours per week. When school is not in session, they can work up to eight hours per day and forty hours per week. While it is not federally required, some states such as Maryland, New York, and Wisconsin require children under eighteen to have a work permit before they can start a job.

Each state has different rules regarding when employees should be paid. Many states, such as California,

Students can work up to forty hours a week when school is not in session. Many work at summer camps or do other work with younger children during the summer.

FAMILY WORK, FARM WORK

Children who are employed by their parents, such as on a farm, do not need to meet the age requirements of the FLSA unless they are working in mining, manufacturing, and other hazardous occupations where the minimum age requirement of eighteen still applies.

Farms that employ children follow different rules than other kinds of employers. The Department of Labor lets farms pay workers under twenty as low as $4.25 per hour. Workers as young as twelve can spend many hours weeding fields and harvesting crops on family or commercial farms. Some of these jobs can be very dangerous, including cleaning inside grain silos.

While more than five hundred thousand children work on their own families' farms in the United States, many children working on farms are migrant workers. Many migrant workers speak English only as a second language and can be taken advantage of by farm owners, which is why the Migrant and Seasonal Agricultural Worker Protection Act (MSPA) helps lay out migrant worker's rights. The MSPA states that workers must be paid the wages they are owed on time and that employers must follow federal safety and health standards if housing is given to workers. It also guarantees that written rules for employment are given to each worker when hired.

allow employers to choose whether to pay workers twice per week (semiweekly), once per week (weekly), or once per month (monthly). Your employer should tell you what payday schedule the company uses when you are hired.

There are some things the FLSA does not cover, including breaks for smoking, holiday pay, pensions, or raises. It also does not cover shift differentials. Individual employers usually set rules for these types of breaks and time-off options. Always make sure you ask for clarity on these issues, which are usually covered in a company handbook. You can also ask the human resources manager at a company or even just your boss or superior.

FILING THE PAPERWORK

When you start a job, there are a variety of forms you must fill out. Most are for tax purposes, so you must be careful with what you sign. Be honest on these forms. Always use your real name, address, and Social Security number.

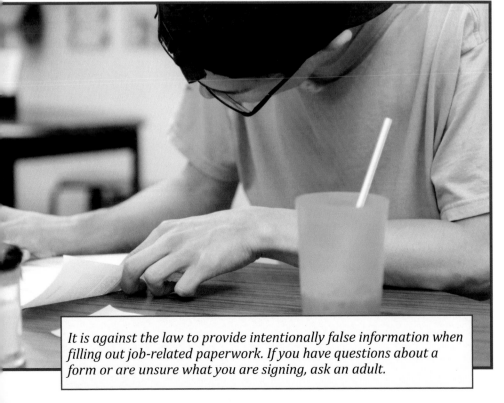

It is against the law to provide intentionally false information when filling out job-related paperwork. If you have questions about a form or are unsure what you are signing, ask an adult.

The I-9 is the Employment Eligibility Verification form, which is used to check your citizenship and other basic information. The W-2 form gives an employer your Social Security number. If you do not have a Social Security number you can apply for one using an S-5 form, which an employer can give to you.

Another form you must fill out tells the Internal Revenue Service (IRS) how much money to take out of your pay as a withholding. Follow the form's instructions to determine whether you want taxes withheld from your paycheck. You can also use the IRS's online withholding allowance calculator.

If you are not required to fill out paperwork for a job, it is possible that your employer hired you illegally. There are many ways employers cheat the tax system, such as hiring employees and giving them W-9 tax forms instead of W-2s. The W-9 form is for freelance workers, who are paid differently and usually don't have taxes taken out of their pay. This means you pay more in taxes at the end of the year while your employer doesn't have to give you basic benefits while on the job. It is illegal to give employees W-9 tax forms unless they are truly self-employed as freelance workers.

Depending on your age, you may need a work permit or other documents to ensure your employment is done legally. If you are hired illegally or paid "under the table," your employer is not paying the proper amount of taxes and you may not be covered by many employee rights. Read each form carefully and ask questions if you are not comfortable with what you are signing. You should also use the

Internet to research what paperwork you are expected to fill out when you start a particular kind of job, or ask a parent or friend for help if you have questions.

Getting "paid under the table," or working without filing tax paperwork, is a common form of unreported employment. This lets employers avoid paying benefits for their employees.

CHAPTER 2

KNOW YOUR RIGHTS

Most jobs have the same basic hiring process. You fill out a job application to apply. If a manager or supervisor looks over your application and believes you are a good candidate for the job, he or she will contact you to set up an interview. The manager may then decide to offer you the position, which you can accept or turn down. Throughout this process it's important to know your rights, not only when filling out an application but also what potential employers are allowed to do during the hiring process.

Employers are supposed to hire employees by looking for the best possible candidate for the job. This means excluding things like age, gender, race, religion, and marital status from their evaluation of potential employees. Some states have even passed laws making it illegal to ask potential employees questions that would reveal their sexual orientation. You should have an equal shot at a position as someone of a different race or gender with the same work experience as you.

The application stage is the point at which you are most likely to be asked about your criminal history. What questions an employer is allowed to ask about whether an applicant has been convicted or arrested vary from state to state. This means it is important to do some research and figure out what the laws in your state are. Some states prohibit employers from asking about arrest records, at least if the arrest is no longer pending or relates to a

Employers are supposed to hire the most qualified person for each position, regardless of race, gender, age, sexual orientation, disability, or any determining factor other than ability to do the job.

juvenile or youth offense. Some states let employers ask about convictions only if they relate directly to the job. Other states require employers who do consider convictions to take particular facts into account, such as the severity of the crime and whether the applicant underwent any rehabilitation. It's also worth remembering that not all offenses are classified as crimes. For example, you may not be obligated to report a violation, such as disorderly conduct or trespassing.

TO TELL THE TRUTH

Many job applications today are submitted online, through a company's website. Some companies even have job seekers fill out applications on computers inside a store rather than hand a paper application to a manager. This lack of face-to-face interaction reduces the chance of a discrimination lawsuit based on physical attributes. Employers can only use information about age or physical ability to exclude people from the hiring process if a "bona fide occupational qualification" exists, which means a trait makes someone unable to do an essential job requirement.

With this in mind, it's important to remember that you have to tell the truth when you are applying for a job. The only question about age an employer can ask on a job application or during an interview is if you are over the age of eighteen. This is to determine the hours and schedule you can work according to the FLSA. Lying about your age is one of the many things you should avoid doing on an application and later during an interview. Never lie about your citizenship or your ability to work either.

Stick to the facts and don't make up any of your job history. You can list volunteer work you have done. Employers want honest workers who are eager to gain job experience. They will hire workers that lack experience if they make a good impression in an interview. Lying on a job application or in an interview could get you fired. It could also stop you from taking legal action against an employer if the employer breaks the law during your employment.

It is important not to lie on a job application, but you should also be aware of any illegal questions on an application that you are not required to answer.

ACING THE INTERVIEW

During an interview, it's your job to sell yourself as a good, reliable worker ready to help make a company better. You should also know the difference between proper and

Confidence is key to any job interview. Show the person interviewing that you are qualified for the job while making sure the interviewer asks fair and legal interview questions.

improper interview questions to make sure your rights aren't violated during the interview process.

Many personal questions often thought of as "small talk" are not actually allowed by employment law. While employers may make judgments based on what you are wearing or whether you are nervous, they are not allowed to ask personal questions about religion or race. Employers can't ask you about your age, where you are from, or if you are disabled. They also can't ask whether you are married or if you have kids. A question such as "Have you ever been arrested?" is illegal, but an employer can ask if you've been convicted of a crime on a job application.

Employers can't ask if you drink socially or whether English is your first language. You should not feel obligated to answer these personal questions because they can help employers learn things about you that they could use to discriminate against you.

If you are asked an improper interview question, there are a few things you can do. The first is to tell the employer that the question they asked is illegal, then refuse to answer it. While this can obviously cause a problem or hurt your chances of getting the job, you can also contact the federal Equal Employment Opportunity Commission (EEOC) and file a claim about the illegal question. If you can honestly answer the question and feel it does not offend you or will not impact your chances of employment, you can answer it.

THE JOB OFFER

After a good interview, you may be offered the job. You do not have to accept the position right away, and you should make sure to check a few things before officially accepting any job offer. A job offer should contain a certain set of things, including a salary and the amount of hours per week you are expected to work. You should also have a clear understanding of what type of work it is and whether it is considered a part-time or full-time job.

Knowing whether the job is part- or full-time can help you understand what kind of benefits come with the employment offer. This includes whether your company will offer you health insurance, dental insurance, or any vision coverage. Benefits can also include any time off. Will you get vacation time? Are there sick or personal days? All of these things should be included in a job offer.

If any of the above are not made clear with the initial job offer, you should ask right away. Clear up any confusion before you accept an offer. When you get a job offer, it is clear that an employer wants you as an employee.

Some jobs offer paid sick days, also known as sick leave. These are days you can take off if you are sick that will not result in any reduction in your paycheck.

TAKING THE TESTS

Some employers have tests for employees to take before they start working. Many of these tests are meant to eliminate people who have employment red flags, such as drug use or past criminal activity. Some retail stores have people take personality tests, which ask a variety of questions about work situations and how potential employees would handle them.

Most employees are not required to take a drug test before they start a job, but companies can make people take tests for a variety of drugs, including marijuana, cocaine, and heroin. Some states, such as California, limit the kinds of drug testing that can be done.

Lie detector tests, also called polygraph tests, are not allowed for most teen jobs. Refusing to take a lie detector test can't prevent you from getting a job, a promotion, or result in any kind of discipline. However, employees can be subject to lie detector tests if an employer thinks the employee was involved in a workplace incident like theft or if an employee will work in security like in an armored car, at a bank, or at a pharmaceutical, or drug, company.

Skills tests are allowed when the test measures a skill necessary for a job, such as typing tests for secretaries. Some jobs have a physical aspect, such as a warehouse job where heavy lifting must be done to complete a job. The Americans with Disabilities Act (ADA) doesn't allow discrimination against people who are disabled or in poor health, so any fitness test must be directly related to a job and its requirements for it to be legal.

21

Now it's your job to make sure you want to work there. Find out what is expected of you and ask any questions you can think of. Take time to think about your decision before jumping into an offer you're not comfortable with. If possible, get the job offer in writing to make sure it includes the salary, benefits, job description, and any other rules discussed with management in it, such as your starting date.

Always read through the employee handbook when you first start a job. You should also occasionally ask for an updated handbook to check if any rules have changed or been added.

Once you accept a job, pay attention to any workplace training you receive during orientation. Part of this process should be an introduction to an employee handbook, which will have more information about what is expected of you at your new job.

While state and federal laws cover many different rules for a workplace, each individual workplace has different rules they expect employees to follow. Read the employee handbook you are given when you start the job. If you are not given one, request one or find out where you can get one. Read all handouts they give you, carefully look over any paperwork you are asked to sign, and be aware of any company programs that can help you should problems occur later. These programs can include anonymous tip lines, suggestion boxes, or other human resources options your company may have set up to help prevent workplace incidents in the future.

Pay attention to any training videos they have you watch. These will explain many employers' policies on a variety of topics, such as proper workplace attire, workplace romances, or even policies such as smoking breaks and vacation time. Knowing the rules your bosses expect you to follow will help limit workplace problems.

GETTING AN INTERNSHIP

One way to get workplace experience before getting a job is to complete an internship. An intern is a person who does work in order to train for a career in a specific field. For example, if you want to become a doctor you could get an internship at a hospital. An aspiring journalist could intern at a newspaper or television station.

Interns are different from regular employees because they usually have a set time period for work: a semester of school or a few months. Many high school–age interns have summer programs that run a few months, between school sessions.

An internship is a great way for students to learn skills and gain knowledge about a particular field in a way they are not able to in the classroom.

Some internships are paid, but many are not. The experience gained during the internship period is considered valuable and often justifies the lack of pay for interns. The U.S. Department of Labor has a six-step test to help employers decide whether their interns should be paid:

1. The training an intern gets is similar to training given in a school.
2. The internship experience benefits the intern.
3. The intern does not replace an employee, but works closely with staff.
4. The employer has no benefit to employing interns over other employees.
5. The intern is not entitled to a job at the end of the internship.
6. Both the employer and intern know there is no pay for the internship.

If the six criteria are met by the internship, then the intern is not entitled to pay. If any of those points are not met, the internship should be paid or the person should be considered a regular employee.

Because interns are not paid employees, they do not have many of the same rights as normal employees. However, the hiring process for interns is often the same as that for regular jobs, with interviews and the same protections against discrimination.

While working in an internship—especially if it is

unpaid—pay attention to what kind of work you are asked to do. If you are doing the exact same job as an actual employee but are not getting a salary, the internship is not legal. Many companies take advantage of interns as a way of obtaining free labor, adding an employee to the company without having to pay or give benefits to the worker. Internships should not be a "trial period" for employers to test out potential employees. If you feel you are being treated unfairly during an internship, tell the intern coordinator at school or talk to management at the internship.

CHAPTER 3

ACCIDENTS AND HARASSMENT

O nce you have a job, it is important to understand your rights, as well as what you must do to make sure your rights are guaranteed to you. When people cross the line in the workplace, there are real consequences to their actions. Whether that discipline comes through a company or law enforcement depends on the severity of the action, but workers should know there are always consequences at work.

One thing to be aware of when dealing with workplace issues is how management reacts to problems. If the people in charge tend to be inflexible, or if they struggle to communicate, it can be difficult to get problems worked out with them. Communication is a complicated process, especially in the workplace. If there are problems management fails to address, it may be time to file complaints on the corporate, state, or federal level.

LEVELS OF VIOLENCE

The threat or act of violence is one of the most dangerous and unpredictable things about a workplace. Whether through physical violence, verbal threats, or unwanted sexual activity, violence has no place in a safe work atmosphere and should be taken very seriously by both employers and employees. According to the Federal

Bureau of Investigation (FBI), there are four main types of workplace violence:

1. Violent acts committed by criminals with no connection to the workplace, such as burglars.

2. Violence directed at employees by customers, patients, students, inmates, or any others who have services provided to them.

3. Violence against coworkers, supervisors, or managers, or by current or former employees.

4. Violence committed by a nonemployees but someone that knows an employee, such as domestic violence committed by an employee's spouse in the workplace.

Not all violence in the workplace involves physical harm. Any threat, whether a verbal or physical one, is a form of violence. Stalking, or following someone and causing fear of harm, is another form of violence. The four kinds of violence outlined by the FBI cover most situations where violence can happen, but violent acts are unpredictable. Simple arguments can turn into physical fighting. Conflict between friends or romantic partners can spill over into the workplace.

There is no surefire way to avoid being exposed to workplace violence, but there are a few general things that can be done to help prevent violence in the workplace. Never escalate any argument or fight. Make sure your workplace has a clear policy about workplace violence so you know what can be done if violent acts occur. This includes a system of record-keeping, a written workplace violence statement, and a program to help employees who become victims of workplace crime. Many state and federal agencies have programs to help employers and employees avoid conflicts in the workplace.

Identifying potential situations for workplace violence can help you prevent any issues from ever causing real harm. When workplace violence happens, whether to you or in your presence, you should report it to your supervisor immediately. Document the behavior, whether in writing or on video. An employer can and should act on this evidence. This action should include a supervisor meeting with the

It's often easy to identify an unsafe situation at work. Loud verbal or physical altercations should always be avoided and reported to supervisors immediately.

workers involved and action to resolve the problem.

If nothing is done to fix the problem, the situation can escalate. This includes arguments with workers or customers, verbal or written threats, or any sort of "revenge," such as vandalism, theft, or any other violation of company rules. When workplace violence escalates, it is important to follow a specific set of rules. First, make sure to secure the safety of yourself and others, especially those who may be in danger. If necessary, call 911 and report the incident to the police. You should also contact your supervisor to report the incident. If possible, document the incident in writing.

The worst types of workplace violence require an emergency response. These include physical fights, suicidal threats, destruction of property, or any incident resulting in extreme anger. The most extreme cases of workplace violence result in physical injury or even death for victims and an arrest for the attacker. If you are a victim of or witness to these extreme acts, you should remain calm and call 911 immediately. Leave the area if your personal safety is at risk, and cooperate with law enforcement to make sure they can work quickly to stop the violence.

Workers have the right to a safe workplace. Any violence or threat of violence should be met with a firm reaction by workers and employers alike. Do not let violence go unanswered, even if an incident doesn't directly involve you. Most crimes against teens happen at school, but 3.2 people in 1,000 experience workplace violence between the age of sixteen and nineteen. Workplace violence is slowly decreasing, but many cases of intimidation and other violent acts still go unreported.

SEXUAL HARASSMENT

Sexual harassment of teens in the workplace has been called an "epidemic" by some experts and is considered a form of violence against employees. One survey of teens working in Maine said one in three were sexually harassed at work. Any workplace should be free of sexual comments, sexual contact, and intimidation. Both males and females can be sexually harassed in the workplace, and many incidents often go unreported.

There are two basic types of sexual harassment claims. The first is "hostile work environment" harassment. This means that a workplace has become uncomfortable, intimidating, or offensive because of sexual harassment. This includes sexual photographs, jokes, threats, and comments from supervisors or workers. If this kind of sexual harassment makes employees want to quit or unable to do their job, they can claim the workplace was too hostile for them to work properly.

The second kind of sexual harassment is sometimes called quid pro quo harassment. "Quid pro quo" is a Latin term that means "something for something." Quid pro quo harassment means someone makes sexual advances or asks for sexual favors in exchange for "rewards" like better pay or a promotion. It can also mean a supervisor threatens to fire an employee for not accepting sexual harassment.

Any sexual harassment should be reported to management so they can act immediately. They should take any action possible to prevent sexual harassment. Make sure employers investigate any claim of harassment seriously. If

Any sexual harassment—whether it leads to a hostile work environ-ment or is quid pro quo sexual harassment—is a serious issue and should be reported immediately.

they do not react to sexual harassment, you can file a claim with the EEOC, who will investigate the claim for you.

Young workers are especially vulnerable to sexual harassment because they do not know what is normal behavior in the workplace. Any discomfort from comments or actions of a coworker or employer should immediately be reported to management. You cannot be punished for reporting sexual harassment. Employers are required to

It's important to define clearly that you are being made uncomfortable or feel you are being harassed. Sexual harassment can come from a superior, a peer, or even a customer.

investigate claims of harassment or can face major lawsuits or other legal action.

BULLIES AND THREATS

According to the Workplace Bullying Institute, up to one in three workers may experience workplace bullying. Bullies are people who tease, hurt, or threaten those who are less powerful. Bullying can come in the form of threats, harassment, intimidation, or other verbal abuse. Often thought of as a problem only in schools, workplace bullying is an everyday issue in a variety of workplaces. Whether it's shouting or swearing at an employee, repeatedly playing practical jokes on someone, or excluding an employee from company activities, workplace bullying can often start with a small action and quickly escalate into a major issue.

It's important to know the difference between bullying and simply being told to do something you don't want to do. Bullying is not being asked to do something job-related that you don't particularly like. It also isn't being forced to work with someone you don't really like. Bullying is a specific action targeting someone with unfair or disrespectful intent.

Bullying can impact a person's physical and mental health. People who have been bullied report problems sleeping, headaches, and stomach issues. They develop lower self-esteem and increased stress. Bullied workers often see their productivity at work decrease and their attendance suffer.

If you feel you are bullied at work, you should talk about the situation with someone you trust. This includes parents or another trusted adult, a friendly coworker, or a teacher. Bullying can be hard to recognize, so it's important to talk with someone about it. Once you know you are being bullied, you can talk with management about the issue or file a workplace complaint with a state or federal labor agency.

Different workplaces have different rules regarding bullying. A company's rules are generally spelled out in its handbook. Some workplaces offer verbal or written warnings or reprimands, sometimes with a system of escalating

Bullying at work can impact more than just how you perform at work. Studies have shown bullying mentally and physically affects one's health.

reprimands for each incident. If your workplace doesn't have a proper system, or you feel your rights are not being protected by your employer, you can contact a workplace lawyer and look into legal action.

Never bully anyone in the workplace. If you feel you have crossed the line into bullying, you should stop immediately and work with your employer to correct

Talking with your parents, friends, or a trusted adult can help you understand how bullying has impacted you. It can also help you take action to resolve any issues you have with bullying at work.

your actions. Bullying in the workplace can lead to serious actions taken against you, including reprimands, the loss of your job, or even civil and legal actions.

WORKPLACE ACCIDENTS

Every nine minutes a teenage worker gets hurt on the job. High shelves at a clothing store, knives or hot cooking equipment in food service, or even stress and back strain at an office job are just a few examples of workplace hazards employees face every day.

It is an employer's job to minimize these hazards by providing employees with safe equipment and offering proper safety training and supervision. Employers must have a plan in place for medical emergencies and provide a first aid kit or other medical help in case of an accident.

The Occupational Safety and Health Act of 1970 set up the Occupational Safety and Health Administration (OSHA), which is a federal agency tasked with enforcing health and safety legislation. OSHA enforces a series of workplace rules that operate to keep workplaces safe for their employees and others. Under OSHA's authority, employers must tell workers about potential job hazards. They must also keep records of workplace accidents and post any OSHA citations on signs where employees can see them.

OSHA has worked for decades to keep workers of all ages safe. The experience helps the agency address common safety risks and hazards in particular fields of work. When working outdoors it's important to watch

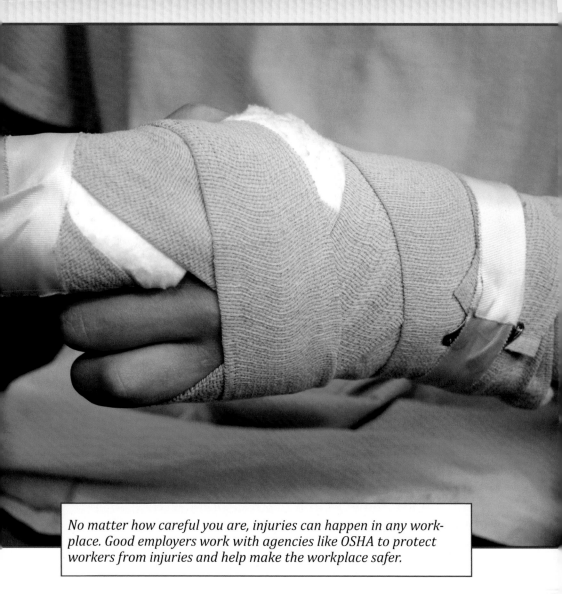

No matter how careful you are, injuries can happen in any workplace. Good employers work with agencies like OSHA to protect workers from injuries and help make the workplace safer.

out for excessive heat or exposure to the sun as well as accidents involving pesticides and chemicals, machinery, electricity, or any heavy lifting. Construction jobs have similar hazards as well as falls and machine or driving accidents. Industrial and agricultural jobs often have

WHISTLEBLOWERS

A whistleblower is someone working at a company who exposes any type of crime or improper things happening there. Anyone who files a formal complaint about these activities is considered a whistleblower, whether that person is concerned about discrimination, workplace safety, or other improper actions by employers or other workers.

Whistleblowers are protected when they file a complaint with OSHA and other agencies. They cannot be disciplined in any way as a reaction to their complaint. This includes being fired or laid off, demoted in any way, "blacklisted" or denied overtime or a promotion, or denied benefits in any way. Whistleblowers cannot be reassigned to a lower position or have their pay or hours reduced as a result of their filing a complaint. They are also protected from threats or intimidation of any sort. Workers can file a discrimination complaint with OSHA within thirty days of an incident that violates whistle-blower protection rules.

hazards with chemicals, noise, and hot or moving equipment.

Working inside at a retail or grocery job brings a variety of hazards, such as heavy lifting and violent crime. Fast food or other food service jobs may also involve sharp objects, hot equipment, and electrical injuries. Even office workers can have issues with repetitive hand movements and neck or back strain.

If you feel your workplace is unsafe, you can file a confidential complaint with OSHA, who will then investigate the claim. OSHA complaints can be filed online, by telephone, and also by mail. If OSHA finds conditions to be hazardous in any way, they can force changes in the workplace to bring conditions up to proper standards.

PRIVACY AT WORK

Workplace privacy is a tough issue, especially when employees work on computers every day. Employers can read the e-mails of employees, track which websites they visit, and even explore the social media pages of workers in order to learn what these employees are doing on company time.

Many companies see these practices as a way to avoid lawsuits. For example, if sexual harassment is happening via e-mail and an employer reads these e-mails, the employer can act on the situation and avoid future legal issues. Do not do anything on a work computer that you wouldn't be comfortable with your boss or your boss's boss seeing. You can be severely reprimanded or even fired for your actions on a computer, especially if you sexually harass or threaten someone.

Employers can listen to your phone calls on work phones, but most are not allowed to listen in on private calls. Some states, such as California, require both sides of a phone conversation to be aware a call is being recorded for it to be legal. This is not the case in other states, such as New York.

Searches of purses and backpacks can occur depending on a company's individual guidelines. Targeted searches, such as those singling out one person for multiple checks, are likely illegal and could be the result of discrimination. Employee monitoring, such as with cameras in the workplace, is also allowed as long as it is not in invasive spaces such as bathrooms or dressing rooms.

An employer can also search a desk, locker, office, or company car because it is considered work property. The same goes for a work computer.

Never bring anything to the workplace or do anything on a work computer you wouldn't want your boss to know about.

CHAPTER 4

CRIMES AND PUNISHMENT

No one wants to be on the receiving end of a workplace crime, but committing a crime or causing an accident can be much worse. There are real consequences to crimes and accidents in the workplace, including fines and jail time. Losing a job over a workplace crime is just the start of a long, difficult journey through the legal system.

Whether you're guilty of a crime or falsely accused, there are a variety of options to explore. Lawyers and others can advocate for you throughout a long journey through the legal system. Knowing whom to turn to and how to defend yourself are important steps as you enter any workplace or criminal investigation. If you are a victim of serious workplace violence, sexual harassment, or rape, you also need to know how to navigate the legal system.

INVESTIGATIONS

Investigations into workplace crime can come from an individual company or a police department. They are launched to find the truth about an incident and punish someone if improper activities are discovered. If you are still working while an investigation is occurring, you must not get distracted by it or tamper with any fact gathering. While cooperating completely with an investigation is generally a good way to avoid drawing attention to your-self, consider talking to an outside attorney to figure out how to protect yourself. It might be worth retaining out-side counsel, or a lawyer who represents you alone and not the whole company. This will help you figure out what your individual liability might be.

You usually have to file an EEOC discrimination charge within 180 days of the incident occurring. An EEOC investigation follows a special protocol that finishes with a

Trying to hide or cover up any wrongdoing could make your punishment worse if the police or your company's human resources department discover any crimes.

definitive ruling about a filed complaint. The EEOC can fine a company money, called punitive damages. A settlement can be agreed upon between the person who filed the complaint and the company, usually through mediation. If this doesn't work, the claimant might be able to seek further legal action, such as a lawsuit.

However, the terms of an employment contract may forbid taking the case to court. This is one reason why it is so important to read your contract completely and to understand its terms. Many large companies, in fact, specifically state that all disputes are to be resolved through private arbitration and not through the courts. This is often done to prevent publicity about the case that a company might otherwise be subject to. There are exceptions that might still let you pursue a lawsuit in a state or federal court, but you should consult an attorney in any event to see what your options are, ideally before you ever enter into a contract.

No matter what route you take when reporting workplace rights violations, make sure to let investigations run their course before taking any further action. The system is designed to help you, and it will if you know your rights.

PAYING THE PRICE

What should you do when you cross the line in the workplace? The easy answer is to stop what you are doing immediately. Whether it's bullying, sexual harassment, stealing, or other violations, you should stop crossing the line right away. Continuing to act improperly or illegally will only make your situation worse. Do not try to hide anything or threaten anyone who will report your actions.

Some improper activities in the workplace will result in reprimands. Others result in the loss of a job, while more severe violations can result in legal action. If you are arrested because of a workplace crime, contact a lawyer immediately. If you cannot afford a lawyer, you will be given a public defender, but a lawyer that specializes in workplace rights can help you the most.

You can be accused of a variety of crimes in the workplace, anything from minor theft to murder. Rape and murder are some of the most serious and severe crimes committed anywhere. Arson is setting fire to property in order to cause severe damage. Theft can be a minor crime for less valuable items, such as petty theft, or a more serious crime like grand larceny.

A wide variety of nonviolent crimes in the workplace are often called "occupational deviance." These include vandalism, drinking on the job, drug use or possession, and misuse of private information.

Punishments for each crime vary by state. The severity of punishment for theft crimes is usually set in each state by a monetary value of what was stolen. Getting convicted of any workplace crime could mean fines, jail time, and a criminal record. It can impact your ability to get employment in the future.

In some cases, you may be sentenced for your workplace crime to a term of probation, rather than jail time. If you violate the terms of your probation, which necessarily include that you do not commit any further crimes and also can involve drug testing and the need to meet regularly with a probation officer, you can be sentenced to jail time.

BUILDING A CASE

Whether you are suing or trying to force action with an employee investigation, it's important to build a strong case for yourself or against your harasser or accuser. The burden of proof is often on you, which means something as simple as keeping proper records can be the difference between winning and losing.

The first thing to do when building a case is to gather credible evidence for your side of the case. This includes documents, pay stubs, notes, and any employee handbooks that are related to your case. If you have a case involving sexual harassment, proof of these crimes can come in the form of any digital or physical evidence of harassment such as text messages, letters, or e-mails. Anything you feel is related to your claim should be saved and organized so it is available if you need it to make your case.

If you think coworkers or supervisors saw your wrongful treatment, they can testify in a courtroom or to other investigative panels about your claims. You should get their names, telephone numbers, and other contact information to make sure they will help you make your case. It is important to make sure these witnesses use facts and help you make a proper case. You should also take note of witnesses that may testify against you in an investigation.

If you are wrongly accused of a crime or in an investigation, you should follow these same steps to build your case against these harmful claims. You should also do your best to defend yourself if you actually committed the crimes you are accused of. No matter your state of guilt or what side of an incident you are on, legal counsel can help you organize your case and work in your best interests in the courtroom and during an investigation.

LAWYERS

Whether you are accused of a crime or bringing a complaint against an abuser, never go into a legal situation without a trained lawyer. Workplace law is a very specific field and can often be very complicated. It's important to have a lawyer familiar with the field that can help you make the best case for your cause.

A lawyer you trust can make a big difference in your case, especially if you are the defendant. You'll also want a lawyer with experience in the legal matters with which you are dealing.

Whether you are battling against a large corporation or an individual, these legal cases often take time, and large companies will have large legal teams to protect their interests. This is why it's important to keep proper records and build a strong case.

Attorneys are usually paid with a retainer, but there are many ways lawyers can be paid. If you can't afford a lawyer, there are many youth rights and workplace rights attorneys who will work pro bono. Finding help in navigating the legal system is an important part of making sure justice is served in your case.

CHAPTER 5

AFTER EMPLOYMENT

No matter what the cause or reason, losing a job is a difficult thing to endure. No matter what happens, it's important to remember there are always new employment opportunities to explore and resources to use to help you through the trying period between jobs.

Each state government has worked hard to ensure options are available for finding employment after termination. So has the federal government. You have basic rights, and unemployment or disability pay may be

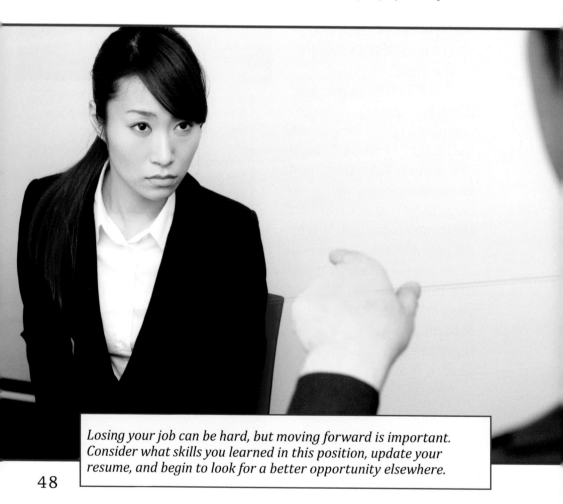

Losing your job can be hard, but moving forward is important. Consider what skills you learned in this position, update your resume, and begin to look for a better opportunity elsewhere.

available to help you bridge the gap between your last employment and your next job.

When you are fired or laid off from a job, federal law says you must get your final paycheck. States have different rules about how and when you will receive your final paycheck. In California, for example, an employer must give you your last paycheck within seventy-two hours of your employment ending. Florida law says a paycheck must be given within six days of being fired or, like in Illinois, on the next scheduled payday.

WRONGFUL TERMINATION

If you don't have an employment contract with your company, you are likely working "at will." This means that your employer doesn't need a reason to fire you. However, an employer can illegally fire employees in a variety of ways. Any termination because of discrimination or retaliation for something such as reporting violence or other incidents protected under whistleblower laws is illegal.

Employers cannot fire you for your age, gender, race, sexual orientation, or any other factor that is used to discriminate. You also cannot lose your job because you formed or were a part of a union or any other use of the legal rights mentioned in this resource. If you feel you were wrongfully fired from a job, you can take legal action against your former employer.

You should not sign any document given to you by your former employee upon your termination without first consulting with an attorney to see how it could impact your rights in regard to bringing a claim against your employer, and what, if anything, you would be sacrificing by signing the agreement.

Your first task to fight against wrongful termination is to document the conditions under which you were fired. You should also keep your employee handbook or any other forms regarding your rights as an employee, which can be used against your company if it broke the law.

Fired employees should contact an employment lawyer who specializes in workplace rights. A lawyer can work with you to examine your claims and see if any action can be taken against an employer. If you feel you were discriminated against, you can also file a complaint with the EEOC.

If you win your case against a former employer, a variety of things can happen depending on the case. Some cases result in a monetary settlement, while others end with a worker getting his or her job back. Back pay, legal fees, and other damages may also be paid to a wrongfully terminated employee.

FINDING A NEW JOB

You can search for another job at any time. Unless you sign an employment contract, you can also leave a job at any time for any reason in the same way that an employer can legally fire any "at-will" worker. It is customary to give employers a full two weeks of notice before starting another job, but there are no formal rules set up by state or federal law. Employers can also terminate contracts, which may give the worker some additional rights and

YOUR CRIMINAL HISTORY

Employers are allowed to ask about your criminal history, but they cannot use this information to discriminate against you. This means that the employer cannot discriminate against employees or potential employees because of their criminal records.

However, there are are important differences between an arrest record and a conviction record. A person can be arrested and never actually convicted of a crime. An arrest record cannot be used to make what's called a "negative employment action," such as not hiring someone, firing an employee, or demoting an employee.

Potential employers can do background checks on job applicants. For some jobs, though, they may need to get the applicants' signed permission first. They also must give you a copy of the report and notify you if a decision to fire, not hire, or not promote you is made based on information in the report.

Again, honesty is the best way to approach your criminal record because lying about past crimes and later having them appear on a criminal history report could be grounds for termination. If you feel the criminal history found in a background check or in another federal database is incorrect, you can file a report with the FBI to challenge your criminal history summary. You can check the status of your state rap sheet by making a request to the court. Likewise, you can request your FBI rap sheet directly from the FBI. If you know there are errors you should immediately seek assistance in getting them corrected.

benefits depending on the type of contract they signed.

It can be tricky to apply for a new job after leaving a previous employer on bad terms. Again, it is important to be as honest as possible on job applications and during interviews. If you were harassed or wrongfully terminated at your previous job, you do not have to explain your situation to a potential employer, but you should not try to hide previous work history.

Even if the termination was your fault, there are always opportunities to find a new job and improve as an employee. Having a positive attitude always helps!

GLOSSARY

attribute A quality belonging to a particular person or thing.

citation An official order or notice from a governing body.

confidential Secret or private.

demote To reduce to a lower rank or job.

deviance Behavior that differs from what is normal or accepted.

discrimination Treating people unequally because of their race, beliefs, age, sex, sexual orientation, or other personal factors.

human resources A branch of a company that deals with the rights and behavior of its employees.

insurance A means of promising protection from something.

liability Being responsible for something according to the law.

mediation Working with two different sides to come to an agreement.

migrant worker A person who moves from place to place following seasonal work, usually on farms.

pension A fixed amount regularly paid to someone after retirement.

pro bono A Latin phrase meaning "for the public good," usually in reference to legal work done at no charge to a client.

protocol A specific set of rules.

public defender A lawyer representing someone who can't afford to hire an attorney.

retainer A payment to secure the services of an attorney, which may either be applied as a flat fee or against hours of work performed.

testify To provide an account under oath.

vandalism The intentional destruction or damage of property.

withholding A deduction of wages taken as an advance payment of income tax.

work permit Legal paperwork needed in some states for youth workers to start a job.

AFL-CIO
815 16th Street NW
Washington, DC 20006
(202) 637-5000
Website: http://www.aflcio.org
The AFL-CIO is a collection of fifty-seven different unions
    that work to protect and grow employee rights in a
    variety of workplaces across the United States.

Canadian Centre for Occupational Health and Safety
135 Hunter Street East
Hamilton, ON L8N 1M5
Canada
(800) 668-4284
Website: http://www.ccohs.ca
This not-for-profit federal department corporation was set
    up in 1978 to provide Canadians with programs that
    promote health and safety in the workplace.

Canadian Labour Program (Toronto office)
Penthouse
4900 Yonge Street
North York, ON M2N 6A4
Canada
(800) 641-4049
Website: http://labour.gc.ca/eng/home.shtml
The Canadian Labour Program is the official employment
    ministry of Canada and can help workers who feel
    their rights have been violated in any Canadian prov-
    ince or territories.

U.S. Department of Labor, Wage and Hour Division
1205 Texas Avenue #607
Lubbock, TX 79401
(886) 487-9243
Website: http://www.dol.gov/whd
The Wage and Hour Division of the U.S. Department of
Labor handles complaints filed against businesses
that are breaking labor laws, including child labor
laws.

Workplace Fairness
920 U Street NW
Washington, DC 20001
(202) 683-6114
Website: http://workplacefairness.org
Workplace Fairness works to ensure employees are aware
of their rights in the workplace, including child labor
laws. They also educate workers about discrimination, harassment, and other workplace problems.

WEBSITES

Because of the changing nature of Internet links, Rosen
Publishing has developed an online list of websites related
to the subject of this book. This site is updated regularly.
Please use this link to access the list:

http://www.rosenlinks.com/KYR/Work

FOR FURTHER READING

Ensaff, Najoud. *Retail Careers*. Mankato, MN: Amicus, 2011.

Floric, Marylee. *Sexual Abuse*. New York, NY: Rosen Central, 2012.

Freedman, Jeri. *Women in the Workplace: Wages, Respect, and Equal Rights*. New York, NY: Rosen Publishing, 2010.

Gillard, Arthur. *Sexual Harassment*. Detroit, MI: Greenhaven Press, 2014.

Haugen, David. *Juvenile Justice*. Detroit, MI: Greenhaven Press, 2013.

Haugen, David. *Labor and Employment*. Detroit, MI: Greenhaven Press, 2013.

Herumin, Wendy. *Child Labor Today: A Human Rights Issue*. Berkeley Heights, NJ: Enslow Publishers, 2008.

Jacobs, Thomas A. *Teens on Trial: Young People Who Challenged the Law—and Changed Your Life*. Minneapolis, MN: Free Spirit Publishing, 2000.

Jacobs, Thomas A. *What Are My Rights? A Q&A About Teens and the Law*. Minneapolis, MN: Free Spirit Publishing, 2011.

Jones, Phil. *Disability Rights*. New York, NY: Chelsea House Publishing, 2012.

Marsico, Katie. *Working on a Farm*. Ann Arbor, MI: Cherry Lake Publishing, 2009.

Murphy, Terry G. *All About Law: Exploring the Canadian Legal System*. Toronto, ON: Nelson Education Limited, 2010.

Pomere, Jonas. *Frequently Asked Questions About Drug Testing*. New York, NY: Rosen Publishing, 2007.

Stearman, Kaye. *Women of Today: Contemporary Issues and Conflicts, 1980–Present*. New York, NY: Chelsea House Publishing, 2011.

Watkins, Heidi. *Teens and Employment*. Detroit, MI: Greenhaven Press, 2011.

Worth, Richard. *Workers' Rights.* Tarrytown, NY: Marshall Cavendish Benchmark, 2008.

BIBLIOGRAPHY

Broder, John M. "Silos Loom as Death Traps on American Farms." *New York Times*, October 28, 2012. Retrieved October 7, 2014 (http://www.nytimes.com/2012/10/29/us/on-us-farms-deaths-in-silos-persist.html?pagewanted=all).

Federal Bureau of Investigations. "Identity History Summary Checks." Retrieved October 7, 2014 (http://www.fbi.gov/about-us/cjis/criminal-history-summary-checks/challenge-of-a-criminal-history-summary).

FindLaw. "Last Paycheck Laws: When Do I Get a Paycheck After Leaving a Job?" Retrieved October 7, 2014 (http://employment.findlaw.com/losing-a-job/last-paycheck-laws.html).

FindLaw. "Whistleblowers." Retrieved October 7, 2014 (http://employment.findlaw.com/whistleblowers.html).

Gunderson, Laura. "Sisters Figure Out the System, Take Allegations Public: Teen Sexual Harassment." *Oregonian*, April 3, 2014. Retrieved October 7, 2014 (http://www.oregonlive.com/business/index.ssf/2014/04/sisters_figure_out_the_system.html).

Gunderson, Laura. "Young Men Increasingly Complain of Workplace Violations: Teen Sexual Harassment." *Oregonian*, April 3, 2014. Retrieved October 7, 2014 (http://www.oregonlive.com/business/index.ssf/2014/04/young_men_increasingly_complai.html).

Gunderson, Laura. "Young Workers Least Likely to Find Help, Yet Suffer Deepest Scars: Teen Sexual Harassment." *Oregonian*, April 1, 2014. Retrieved October 7, 2014 (http://www.oregonlive.com/business/index.ssf/2014/04/teen_sexual_harassment_victimi.html).

Korn, Melissa. "True or False: These Tests Can Tell if You Are Right for This Job." *Wall Street Journal*, October 29, 2012. Retrieved October 7, 2014 (http://online.

wsj.com/news/articles/SB10000872396390444812
704577609413668058818).

Lucas, Suzanne. "Can I Leave a Job Off My Resume?" cbsnews.com, September 6, 2013. Retrieved October 7, 2014 (http://www.cbsnews.com/news/can-i-leave-a-job-off-my-resume/).

Nolo.com. "California Laws on Drug Testing." Retrieved October 7, 2014 (http://www.nolo.com/legal-encyclopedia/california-laws-drug-testing.html).

Seattle City Council. "City Council Approves $15/hour Minimum Wage in Seattle." June 2. Retrieved October 7, 2014 (http://www.seattle.gov/council/issues/minimumwage/default.html).

Tahmincioglu, Eve. "Many Teens Face Sexual Harassment on the Job." NBCNews.com, June 7, 2010. Retrieved October 7, 2014 (http://www.nbcnews.com/id/37320747/ns/business-careers/t/many-teens-face-sexual-harassment-job/#.VAagwGSwIz4).

Tam, Jessica. "What Is Required While on Supervised Probation?" Legalmatch.com, September 17, 2013. Retrieved October 7, 2014 (http://www.legalmatch.com/law-library/article/what-is-required-while-on-supervised-probation.html)

Texas Workplace Commission. "Workplace Investigations — Basic Issues for Employers." Retrieved October 7, 2014 (http://www.twc.state.tx.us/news/efte/workplace_investigations_basics.html).

U.S. Department of Justice, Bureau of Justice Statistics. "Special Report: Workplace Violence, 1993–2009." March 2011. Retrieved October 7, 2014 (http://www.bjs.gov/content/pub/pdf/wv09.pdf).

U.S. Department of Justice, Federal Bureau of Investigation. "Workplace Violence: Issues in Response." 2004. Retrieved October 7, 2014 (http://www.fbi.gov/stats-services/publications/workplace-violence).

U.S. Department of Labor, Occupational Safety & Health Division. "Young Workers: You Have Rights!" Retrieved October 7, 2014 (https://www.osha.gov/youngworkers).

U.S. Department of Labor, Wage and Hour Division. "Basic Information." June 2012. Retrieved October 7, 2014 (http://www.dol.gov/whd/regs/compliance/whd_fs.pdf).

U.S. Department of Labor, Wage and Hour Division. "Fact Sheet #71: Internship Programs Under the Fair Labor Standards Act." April 2010. Retrieved October 7, 2014 (http://www.dol.gov/whd/regs/compliance/whdfs71.htm).

Williams, Joseph. "My Life as a Retail Worker: Nasty, Brutish, and Poor." *The Atlantic*, March 11, 2014. Retrieved October 7, 2014 (http://www.theatlantic.com/business/archive/2014/03/my-life-as-a-retail-worker-nasty-brutish-and-poor/284332/).

Williams, Ray B. "The Silent Epidemic: Workplace Bullying." *Psychology Today*, May 3, 2011. Retrieved October 7, 2014 (http://www.psychologytoday.com/blog/wired-success/201105/the-silent-epidemic-workplace-bullying).

INDEX

ABOUT THE AUTHOR

Ryan Nagelhout is a children's author who lives in Niagara Falls, New York. He has a B.A in communication studies with a concentration in journalism from Canisius College in Buffalo, New York. A former newspaper reporter in Niagara Falls, he now works in the publishing industry.

ABOUT THE EXPERT REVIEWER

Lindsay A. Lewis, Esq., is a practicing criminal defense attorney in New York City, where she handles a wide range of matters, from those discussed in this series to high-profile federal criminal cases. She believes that each and every defendant deserves a vigorous and informed defense. Lewis is a graduate of the Benjamin N. Cardozo School of Law and Vassar College.

PHOTO CREDITS

Cover © iStockphoto.com/KatarzynaBialasiewicz; cover (background), p. 1 Christophe Rolland/Shutterstock.com; pp. 5, 15 Photofusion/ Universal Images Group/Getty Images; pp. 6–7 Erik Dreyer/The Image Bank/Getty Images; p. 9 kali9/E+/Getty Images; p. 11 PamelaJoeMcFarlane/E+/Getty Images; p. 13 PhotoAlto/EricAudras/ Getty Images; p. 17 MachineHeadz/E+/Getty Images; p. 18 weareadventurers/iStock/Thinkstock; p. 20 Mixa/Getty Images; p. 22 michaelquirk/iStock/Thinkstock; pp. 24–25 Hero Images/Getty Images; p. 29 Joos Mind/The Image Bank/Getty Images; p. 32 MivPiv/E+/Getty Images; p. 33 Zero Creatives/Cultura/Getty Images; p. 35 Creatista/ Shutterstock.com; pp. 36–37 Jose Luis Pelaez/Blend Images/Getty Images; p. 38 Frances Twitty/E+/Getty Images; p. 41 Peter Dazeley/ Photographer's Choice/Getty Images; p. 43 Monty Rakusen/Cultura/ Getty Images; p. 47 Stockbyte/Getty Images; pp. 48–49 Miyuki/Getty Images; pp. 52–53 Izabela Habur/E+/Getty Images.

Designer: Brian Garvey; Editor: Amelie von Zumbusch